Daughter Of The King: Embracing Your Identity In Christ

Joshua Rhoades

Published by Joshua Paul Rhoades, 2024.

DAUGHTER OF THE KING: EMBRACING YOUR IDENTITY IN CHRIST

First edition. September 20, 2024.

Copyright © 2024 Joshua Rhoades.

ISBN: 979-8224025909

Written by Joshua Rhoades.

Also by Joshua Rhoades

Courage Under Fire: David's Stand On The Battlefield

Jonah's Journey: Voices Of Redemption And Lessons In Obedience

The Furnace Of Faith: 12 Principles From The Heat Of Faith

Whispers of Hope: Inspiring Stories of Men's Prayers In Scripture

Frontier Legends: The Oregon Dream

Elijah: A Beacon Of Boldness

HOOK, LINE & SAVIOUR - Faith Reflections from Fishing

Driven By Faith: Motor Racing Inspired Christian Life

30 Day Devotional - Bold and Strong- Coffee Devotions for a Courageous Christian Walk

Authentic Christianity: The Heart of Old Time Religion

Consider The Ant - God's Tiny Preachers

Flee Fornication: The Plea For Purity

Renewed Hope- How to Find Encouragement in God

Sounding The Call - The Voice of Conviction

The Altar - Where Heaven Meets Earth

The Bible's Battlefields- Timeless Lessons from Ancient Wars

The Sacred Art of Silence - How Silence Speaks in Scripture

Under Fire- The Sanctity of the Traditional Biblical Home

Who Is on the Lord's Side? A Call to Righteousness

What Is Truth? - From Skepticism to Submission

First and Goal- Faith and Football Fundamentals

From Dugout to Devotion- Spiritual Lessons from Baseball

Par for the Course- Faith and Fairways

The Believer's Pace- Tools for Running Life's Marathon

The Immutable Fortress- Security in God's Unchanging Nature

Biblical Bravery

Deer Stands and Devotions: A Hunter's Walk with God

Dedication

To the young lady who has given her heart to Jesus and is ready to live a life that honors Him: this dedication is for you.

You've made the most important decision you'll ever make—choosing to follow Jesus Christ. Now, you stand at the beginning of an incredible journey. You are not just any young woman; you are a daughter of the King. You belong to Jesus, the King of Kings, and this identity will shape the rest of your life. But with that identity comes responsibility, courage, and a calling. This isn't always an easy path, but it is one that leads to joy, purpose, and eternal fulfillment.

You are called to live differently because you are different. The world may try to pull you in every direction, telling you how to live, how to look, and who to be. But remember, you are not defined by what the world says. You are defined by the One who created you and gave His life for you. The world may tell you that beauty, success, and popularity are what matter, but as a daughter of the King, you know that your worth is not found in those things. Your worth is found in the fact that Jesus loves you unconditionally, has chosen you, and has called you to live for Him.

Living for the Lord requires strength and courage. There will be moments when standing for what's right will make you stand alone. There will be times when doing what God asks will make you feel like you're swimming against the current. But take heart, for God has not left you to do this on your own. He has given you His Spirit to empower you, His Word to guide you, and His love to sustain you. When the world tries to dim your light, let the truth that you are a daughter of the King shine even brighter.

You are part of something much bigger than yourself. As a daughter of the King, you are a representative of Christ to the world. When others see you, they should see the love of Jesus in your actions, the humility of Christ in your attitude, and the truth of the gospel in your words. This is no small task, but it is a beautiful privilege. You are a light in the darkness, a beacon of hope in a world that desperately needs to see the love of Christ.

In those moments when you feel weak, remember that your strength comes from the Lord. When you feel uncertain, know that God has a plan and a purpose for your life. When you feel unloved, remember that you are deeply and eternally loved by the One who gave His life for you.

This dedication is to remind you that you are not ordinary. You are royalty, chosen by God to be His daughter. Walk in that truth every day, live boldly for Him, and never forget that you are loved beyond measure by the King of Kings.

This journey will be challenging, but it will be worth it. So, dear daughter of the King, live your life for the glory of the One who has called you, and let your light shine for Him in all you do.

Introduction

Every young woman is searching for her identity—who she is, what defines her, and where she truly belongs. In a world that constantly tells you who you should be, how you should look, and what you should accomplish, it's easy to feel overwhelmed, confused, or lost. The pressure to fit into society's mold is accurate, and sometimes, it can seem impossible to know your true worth. But the truth is, your identity is not found in the world's ever-changing standards. Your identity is found in something much more significant: you are a daughter of the King.

Being a daughter of the King means that you belong to God, the Creator of the universe, the One who loves you unconditionally and who has chosen you to be His own. This title is not based on anything you have done but on what Christ has done for you. Through His sacrifice, you have been adopted into God's family, and you are now His beloved daughter with all the rights, privileges, and promises that come with being part of His kingdom. Embracing this identity changes everything. It shifts your focus from trying to meet the world's expectations to resting in the security of God's love and purpose for your life.

"Daughter of the King: Embracing Your Identity in Christ" is an invitation to discover who you are in Christ. This book is not just about learning facts; it's about experiencing a deep, personal relationship with the One who calls you His own. It's about understanding that your worth is not defined by your appearance, achievements, or what others think of you. Instead, your worth is determined by the God who created you, redeemed you, and called you, His daughter. This truth brings freedom—freedom from the comparison trap, the fear of not being enough, and the need to prove yourself constantly.

In this book, you will explore what it means to live as a daughter of the King in every aspect of your life. You will be guided to embrace your God-given identity through Scripture, practical insights, and personal reflection. You will learn to see yourself through God's eyes, live out your purpose confidently, and walk in the freedom, joy, and peace that comes from knowing who you are in Christ.

As a daughter of the King, you have a royal calling. You are chosen, loved, and set apart for a life that glorifies God. You are called to shine His light in the world, to love others with His love, and to reflect His character in everything you do. This is not a burden but a privilege. As you embrace your identity in Christ, you will discover the strength, grace, and purpose that God has given you to live out your calling.

So, are you ready to fully step into your identity as a daughter of the King? This journey will be transformative, and it starts with understanding one simple truth: you are loved, you are chosen, and you belong to the King of kings. Let's begin.

Chapter 1 - Maintain a Pure Heart

For a young lady who desires to live for the Lord, one of the most important lessons she can learn is the value of maintaining a pure heart. In the Bible, the heart represents the center of our emotions, thoughts, and desires. It is the core of who we are and affects everything we do. Having a clean and pure heart before Him is essential to live a life that pleases God. Psalm 51:10 says, "Create in me a clean heart, O God; and renew a right spirit within me." This verse shows the importance of seeking God to purify our hearts because, without His help, we can easily be led astray by negative influences, selfish desires, or sin. A pure heart doesn't come naturally, but it is something we must continually ask God to create in us. When our hearts are pure, we can live in a way that honors God, reflects His love, and leads us to make choices that align with His will.

The idea of guarding our hearts is also emphasized in Proverbs 4:23, which instructs us to "Keep thy heart with all diligence; for out of it are the issues of life." This verse is a reminder that the condition of our hearts affects every area of our lives. Whether it's the way we think, the way we speak, or the way we act, everything flows from the heart. If our hearts are filled with things that don't honor God, such as bitterness, envy, or selfishness, it will show how we live. On the other hand, if we fill our hearts with love, kindness, and godly wisdom, our lives will reflect those qualities. Guarding our hearts requires intentionality. We must be careful about what we allow into our hearts and minds, whether through what we watch, listen to, or the people we surround ourselves with. Negative influences can easily pull us away from God's path, but by diligently guarding our hearts, we can stay focused on living a life that pleases Him.

For a young lady who desires to live for the Lord, having a pure heart means letting God search her heart and reveal any areas that need to change. It means being humble enough to admit she's wrong and seeking forgiveness when she falls short. Psalm 139:23-24 says, "Search me, O God, and know my heart: try me, and know my thoughts: and see if there be any wicked way in me, and lead me in the way everlasting." These verses show the importance of regularly inviting God to examine our hearts and guide us in the right direction. Keeping a pure heart is not a one-time event but a lifelong process of allowing God to work in us and cleanse us from anything that doesn't align with His will.

Maintaining a pure heart also involves letting go of bitterness, anger, and unforgiveness. These negative emotions can take root in our hearts and block us from experiencing the fullness of God's love and peace. In Ephesians 4:31-32, we are told, "Let all bitterness, and wrath, and anger, and clamour, and evil speaking, be put away from you, with all malice: and be ye kind one to another, tenderhearted, forgiving one another, even as God for Christ's sake hath forgiven you." By forgiving others and letting go of grudges, we can free our hearts from negativity and open ourselves to the love and grace God wants to pour into our lives.

In addition to guarding against negative emotions, maintaining a pure heart also means being mindful of our thoughts. Our thoughts shape our attitudes, and our attitudes shape our actions. Philippians 4:8 encourages us to focus on genuine, honorable, just, pure, lovely, and commendable things. By filling our minds with positive and godly thoughts, we can keep our hearts pure and stay on God's path. It's easy to get caught up in negative thinking or to dwell on things that don't matter, but God calls us to set our minds on things above and to focus on what is good and pure.

Living with a pure heart is about more than just avoiding sin; it's about actively pursuing God's will and His righteousness. In Matthew 5:8, Jesus says, "Blessed are the pure in heart: for they shall see God." This beatitude reminds us that when we strive to keep our hearts pure, we can see and experience God's presence. A pure heart allows us to have a deeper relationship with God and to hear His voice more clearly. It helps us to discern His will for our lives and to walk in obedience to His Word.

For a young lady who wants to live for the Lord, maintaining a pure heart also means being careful about the company she keeps. 1 Corinthians 15:33 warns, "Be not deceived: evil communications corrupt good manners." The people we surround ourselves with have a significant influence on our hearts and our actions. Keeping our hearts pure becomes much more challenging if we spend time with those who lead us away from God or encourage us to make poor choices. However, by surrounding ourselves with godly friends who inspire us in our walk with the Lord, we can stay focused on living a life that pleases Him.

One of the best ways to maintain a pure heart is through prayer and regular time in God's Word. When we pray, we invite God into every area of our lives, including our hearts. We ask Him to cleanse, guide, and help us make decisions that align with His will. Prayer is a powerful tool for keeping our hearts connected to God and ensuring we stay on the right path. In addition to prayer, spending time in the Bible helps us to fill our minds and hearts with God's truth. The more we immerse ourselves in Scripture, the more we will be able to recognize what is pure and right, and the easier it will be to avoid the things that lead us astray.

Maintaining a pure heart doesn't mean we will never make mistakes or get everything right. Sometimes, we fall short, but the key is to return to God and ask for His forgiveness and grace to start anew. Lamentations 3:22-23 reminds us that "It is of the Lord's mercies that we are not consumed, because his compassions fail not. They are new every morning: great is thy faithfulness." God's mercy is new every day, and He is always ready to forgive us and help us get back on track. No matter how often we stumble, God is faithful in helping us maintain a pure heart when we seek Him sincerely.

Living with a pure heart is a daily commitment. It requires us to be intentional about our choices, the thoughts we entertain, and the influences we allow into our lives. But when we keep our hearts pure before God, we experience the incredible joy and peace of walking in His ways. Psalm 24:3-4 asks, "Who shall ascend into the hill of the Lord? or who shall stand in his holy place? He that hath clean hands, and a pure heart." A pure heart allows us to draw closer to God and stand in His presence; there is no more tremendous blessing.

In conclusion, maintaining a pure heart is essential for a young lady who desires to live for the Lord. It is the foundation of a life that pleases God and reflects His love for the world. By guarding her heart against negative influences, choosing to forgive, filling her mind with godly thoughts, surrounding herself with positive influences, and staying connected to God through prayer and Scripture, she can keep her heart pure and live a life that honors Him. While the journey may not always be easy, God's grace is sufficient, and His mercies are new every morning. As she continues to seek Him with a sincere and pure heart, she will experience the fullness of His love, His peace, and His guidance in her life.

Chapter 2 - Meditate on God's Word

For a young lady who desires to live for the Lord, one of the most important habits she can develop is to meditate on God's Word daily. The Bible is not just an ordinary book but God's living Word, full of wisdom, guidance, and truth. It can shape our thoughts, transform our hearts, and guide our actions. When we make time each day to meditate on Scripture, we allow God's Word to become the foundation of our lives, influencing everything we do and every decision we make. Psalm 1:2 tells us, "But his delight is in the law of the Lord; and in his law doth he meditate day and night." This verse shows us the joy and blessing of consistently meditating on God's Word. Meditating on Scripture means more than just reading it—it means profoundly reflecting on its meaning, letting it sink into our hearts and minds, and thinking about how we can apply it to our daily lives. Meditating on God's Word day and night allows it to guide our thoughts, shape our attitudes, and direct our actions.

Meditating on God's Word requires intentionality. It's easy to get caught up in the busyness of life, with school, friends, family, and other responsibilities taking up our time and attention. But to live for the Lord, we must prioritize meditating on Scripture. Joshua 1:8 instructs us, "This book of the law shall not depart out of thy mouth; but thou shalt meditate therein day and night, that thou mayest observe to do according to all that is written therein: for then thou shalt make thy way prosperous, and then thou shalt have good success." This verse reminds us that meditating on God's Word is essential for living a successful and prosperous life—not in the worldly sense of fame or fortune, but in the spiritual sense of living a life that pleases God and reflects His glory. When we meditate on God's Word, we allow it to shape our decisions, relationships, and attitudes, helping us live in a way that honors Him.

One of the critical benefits of meditating on Scripture is that it helps us to stay focused on God throughout the day. In a world of distractions, losing sight of what matters is easy. We are constantly bombarded with messages from social media, entertainment, and other sources that can pull us away from God's truth. But when we take time each day to meditate on Scripture, we are grounding ourselves in God's Word and reminding ourselves of His promises and commands. Colossians 3:16 encourages us to "Let the word of Christ dwell in you richly in all wisdom." When God's Word dwells in us richly, it becomes a source of strength and guidance, helping us navigate life's challenges with wisdom and grace.

Meditating on God's Word also helps us to guard our hearts and minds against negative influences. Philippians 4:8 tells us, "Finally, brethren, whatsoever things are true, whatsoever things are honest, whatsoever things are just, whatsoever things are pure, whatsoever things are lovely, whatsoever things are of good report; if there be any virtue, and if there be any praise, think on these things." Meditating on Scripture fills our minds with true, pure, and lovely things, protecting us from the world's lies and temptations. It's easy to get caught up in negative thinking or dwell on things harmful to our spiritual growth, but when we meditate on God's Word, we set our minds on good and righteous things. This helps us maintain a pure heart and a focused mind, essential for living a life that honors God.

Another benefit of meditating on God's Word is that it helps us to know God more deeply. The Bible is God's revelation to us—His way of communicating His character, His will, and His love for us. When we meditate on Scripture, we are not just reading words on a page; we are getting to know the heart of God. Psalm 119:105 says, "Thy word is a lamp unto my feet, and a light unto my path." God's Word illuminates the path before us, showing us who He is and how we can follow Him. Meditating on Scripture teaches us more about God's holiness, mercy, justice, and grace. This deepens our relationship with Him and helps us to trust Him more fully in every area of our lives.

Meditating on God's Word also equips us to stand firm in our faith, especially when we face challenges or difficulties. Life is full of trials, and we are not immune to hardship as Christians. But when we meditate on Scripture, we are reminded of God's promises and His faithfulness. Romans 8:28 reassures us, "And we know that all things work together for good to them that love God, to them who are the called according to his purpose." By meditating on verses like this, we can find comfort and hope in trials, knowing that God is in control and working all things for our good. When we meditate on God's Word, we are better equipped to face life's challenges with confidence and peace, trusting that God will never leave or forsake us.

Another essential aspect of meditating on God's Word is that it helps us to discern right from wrong. A solid foundation of truth is crucial in a world that often blurs the lines between good and evil. Hebrews 4:12 tells us, "For the word of God is quick, and powerful, and sharper than any two-edged sword, piercing even to the dividing asunder of soul and spirit, and of the joints and marrow, and is a discerner of the thoughts and intents of the heart." God's Word can reveal the truth, expose sin, and guide us in making decisions that honor Him. When we meditate on Scripture, we sharpen our ability to discern what is right and proper, which helps us to live according to God's standards rather than the world's.

Meditating on God's Word also strengthens our faith. Romans 10:17 says, "So then faith cometh by hearing, and hearing by the word of God." The more we meditate on Scripture, the more our faith grows. When we reflect on God's promises, faithfulness, and love, our trust in Him deepens, and our faith becomes more substantial. This is especially important when we face doubts or uncertainties. By meditating on God's Word, we can remind ourselves of His past faithfulness and unchanging nature, which gives us the confidence to trust Him in the present and the future.

One of the most practical ways to meditate on God's Word is to memorize Scripture. Psalm 119:11 says, "Thy word have I hid in mine heart, that I might not sin against thee." Memorizing Scripture allows us to carry God's Word wherever we go, even when we don't have a Bible. It helps us to recall God's truth in moments of temptation, fear, or doubt. By committing verses to memory, we build a reservoir of truth that we can draw from in any situation. Whether facing a difficult decision, dealing with stress, or needing encouragement, having Scripture hidden in our hearts allows us to meditate on God's Word throughout the day and let it guide our thoughts and actions.

Meditating on God's Word is not just about personal growth; it also equips us to share God's truth with others. 1 Peter 3:15 encourages us to "be ready always to give an answer to every man that asketh you a reason of the hope that is in you." Meditating on Scripture prepares us to share the gospel and explain our faith to others. God's Word gives us the wisdom and knowledge to be effective witnesses for Christ. As we meditate on Scripture, we are growing in our faith and becoming better equipped to lead others to the truth of God's Word.

In conclusion, meditating on God's Word is vital for any young lady who desires to live for the Lord. Psalm 1:2 and Joshua 1:8 remind us of the importance of meditating on Scripture day and night, allowing it to shape our thoughts, guide our actions, and transform our hearts. By making time each day to reflect on God's Word, we can stay focused on Him, guard our hearts against negative influences, grow in our knowledge of His character, strengthen our faith, and discern right from wrong. Meditating on Scripture also equips us to face life's challenges confidently, share God's truth with others, and deepen our relationship with Him. As we commit to meditating on God's Word, we will experience the incredible blessings of living a life rooted in His truth and guided by His wisdom. Let us make it a daily habit to meditate on Scripture, allowing God's Word to dwell richly in our hearts and to lead us in every area of our lives.

Chapter 3 - Make Wise Choices

As a young person growing up and trying to navigate the world, making wise choices is vital. Our big or small decisions have lasting consequences, shaping our future, relationships, and faith. The Bible emphasizes the importance of seeking God's wisdom in every decision, knowing that true wisdom comes from the Lord. Proverbs 3:5-6 teaches us, "Trust in the Lord with all thine heart; and lean not unto thine own understanding. In all thy ways acknowledge him, and he shall direct thy paths." This verse is a powerful reminder that our understanding is often limited, and we must trust God's guidance. When we rely solely on our thoughts and desires, we can easily make choices that lead us down the wrong path, but when we seek God's wisdom and trust Him completely, He promises to direct our paths, helping us make decisions that honor Him and lead to a life filled with purpose and fulfillment.

One of our greatest gifts as believers is asking God for wisdom whenever needed. James 1:5 encourages us by saying, "If any of you lack wisdom, let him ask of God, that giveth to all men liberally, and upbraideth not; and it shall be given him." This verse tells us that whenever we face a decision, no matter how difficult or confusing it may seem, we can always turn to God and ask Him for the wisdom we need. The best part is that God gives His wisdom generously to those who ask. He doesn't hold back or criticize us for not knowing what to do. Instead, He is eager to provide the guidance we need to make choices that reflect His will and bring glory to Him. Making wise choices isn't about being perfect or never making mistakes—it's about seeking God's direction, listening to His voice, and trusting He knows what is best for us.

When making wise choices, it's essential to understand that wisdom goes beyond knowing right or wrong. Wisdom is about applying the knowledge we have in a way that honors God and benefits ourselves and others. Proverbs 9:10 says, "The fear of the Lord is the beginning of wisdom: and the knowledge of the holy is understanding." True wisdom starts with a deep reverence and respect for God. When we fear the Lord, we acknowledge that He is the source of all truth, and we desire to live in a way that pleases Him. This wisdom guides every aspect of our lives, from how we treat others to our decisions about our future. As we grow in wisdom, we learn to see things from God's perspective and make choices that align with His plan for our lives.

Making wise choices also involves being careful about the influences we allow into our lives. In today's world, countless voices compete for our attention—whether through social media, television, friends, or other sources. Not all of these voices lead us in the right direction. Proverbs 13:20 warns us, "He that walketh with wise men shall be wise: but a companion of fools shall be destroyed." The people we surround ourselves with and the influences we listen to significantly shape our choices. If we spend time with people who make poor choices, it's easy to follow their lead and make decisions that take us away from God's path. But if we surround ourselves with people who seek God's wisdom and live according to His Word, we are more likely to make wise choices that bring honor to Him. We must seek out friendships and relationships that encourage us to grow in our faith and help us stay on the right path.

One of the most important aspects of making wise choices is learning to be patient and not rush into decisions. Proverbs 19:2 warns us, "Also, that the soul is without knowledge, it is not good; and he that hasteth with his feet sinneth." This verse reminds us that when we make decisions hastily, without seeking God's wisdom or considering the consequences, we are more likely to make mistakes. It's essential to pray, seek counsel from others, and wait for the Lord's direction before making big decisions. Sometimes, we may feel pressured to make a quick choice, but wisdom teaches us to be patient and trust that God's timing is always perfect. When we wait on the Lord, we allow Him to guide us in the right direction and reveal His plans.

Another key to making wise choices is learning from our mistakes. None of us are perfect, and there will be times when we make decisions that don't turn out the way we hoped. But even in those moments, God can teach us valuable lessons if we listen and learn. Proverbs 3:11-12 encourages us, "My son, despise not the chastening of the Lord; neither be weary of his correction: for whom the Lord loveth he correcteth; even as a father the son in whom he delighteth." When we make a wrong choice and face the consequences, it's important to remember that God's correction expresses His love for us. He doesn't want us to continue down the wrong path, so He lovingly guides us back to where we need to be. Making wise choices means being humble enough to admit when we've made a mistake, seeking God's forgiveness, and asking Him to help us make better decisions in the future.

It's also important to remember that making wise choices often requires courage. There will be times when doing the right thing is difficult or unpopular. We may face pressure from others to compromise our values or to make choices that go against God's Word. But wisdom teaches us to stand firm in our faith, even when it's hard. Joshua 1:9 reminds us, "Have not I commanded thee? Be strong and of a good courage; be not afraid, neither be thou dismayed: for the Lord thy God is with thee whithersoever thou goest." When we trust in God's wisdom and rely on His strength, we can make choices that honor Him, even in the face of opposition or difficulty. God is always with us and will give us the courage to stand for what is right.

Making wise choices also means being mindful of the long-term consequences of our decisions. Proverbs 14:12 warns, "There is a way which seemeth right unto a man, but the end thereof are the ways of death." Sometimes, a choice may seem reasonable, but if we don't take the time to consider the long-term effects, we may face unintended consequences. Wisdom teaches us to consider our choices impact on our future, relationships, and walk with the Lord. By seeking God's guidance and evaluating the long-term effects, we can make decisions that lead to life rather than choices that bring harm or regret.

In addition to seeking God's wisdom through prayer and His Word, it's also wise to seek counsel from godly mentors and leaders. Proverbs 11:14 tells us, "Where no counsel is, the people fall: but in the multitude of counsellors there is safety." God often uses the wisdom of others to help guide us in making wise choices. Whether it's a parent, pastor, teacher, or trusted friend, it's essential to seek advice from people who are strong in their faith and can offer biblical wisdom. Sometimes, others can see things differently or point out potential pitfalls we may have missed. By seeking wise counsel, we can gain valuable insight that helps us make decisions that honor God and lead us in the right direction.

Finally, making wise choices is about trusting God with the outcome of our decisions. Sometimes, we may feel uncertain or anxious about the future, but Proverbs 16:9 reminds us, "A man's heart deviseth his way: but the Lord directeth his steps." When we seek God's wisdom and make decisions based on His guidance, we can trust that He will direct our steps and lead us where we need to go. Even if things don't turn out exactly as planned, we can have confidence that God is in control and working all things for our good. Making wise choices is ultimately about surrendering our will to God and trusting His plans are better than our own.

In conclusion, making wise choices is a vital part of living a life that honors God. Proverbs 3:5-6 and James 1:5 remind us of the importance of seeking God's wisdom in every big and small decision. By trusting in the Lord with all our hearts, seeking His guidance, and asking Him for wisdom, we can make choices that reflect His will and lead to a life filled with purpose and blessing. Wisdom teaches us to be patient, to consider the long-term consequences of our decisions, to seek godly counsel, and to trust God with the outcome. While making wise choices isn't always easy, it is possible when we rely on God's strength, His Word, and His wisdom. As we grow in our relationship with Him, we can be confident that He will guide us in making decisions that lead to a life that brings glory to His name. Let us seek God's wisdom in every area of our lives, trusting He will direct our paths and lead us in righteousness.

Chapter 4 - Modesty in Appearance and Behavior

Modesty in appearance and behavior is one of the most essential principles for a young lady who desires to live a life that honors God. In today's world, where so much emphasis is placed on outward beauty and self-expression, it can be easy to get caught up in what we wear, how we present ourselves, and how others perceive us. However, the Bible teaches that true beauty and worth come not from what we wear or look but from the condition of our hearts and conduct. Modesty is not just about our clothes—it's about reflecting a heart that seeks to honor God in every area of life, from our appearance to our words and actions.

1 Timothy 2:9 encourages women to "adorn themselves in modest apparel, with shamefacedness and sobriety." This verse is often used when discussing the importance of dressing modestly, but it goes beyond that. Modesty in this context refers to more than what we wear—it is about having an attitude of humility, respect, and self-control. "Shamefacedness" refers to a sense of humility and reverence, being mindful of how our actions reflect our faith and how we present ourselves to others. "Sobriety" means having self-control and being aware of how we dress and behave, making sure that we do not draw unnecessary attention to ourselves or act in a way that distracts from our relationship with God. Dressing modestly and behaving with dignity shows that our identity is rooted in Christ, not the world's beauty standards or approval.

Modesty in appearance is important because it reflects the condition of our hearts. 1 Peter 3:3-4 reminds us that true beauty comes not from outward appearances but from the "hidden man of the heart." The passage says, "Whose adorning let it not be that outward adorning of plaiting the hair, and of wearing of gold, or of putting on of apparel; But let it be the hidden man of the heart, in that which is not corruptible, even the ornament of a meek and quiet spirit, which is in the sight of God of great price." These verses emphasize that while outward appearance can reflect our character, our inner spirit—our heart—truly matters to God. A heart that is humble, gentle, and focused on pleasing God is more valuable than any outward display of beauty or fashion.

Living modestly means making choices that align with God's standards rather than the world's. It means being mindful of how we dress, speak, and behave in all situations. In today's culture, there is often pressure to dress in a way that seeks attention or validation from others, whether through revealing clothing or flashy trends. But the Bible calls us to a higher standard. Modesty in appearance means choosing respectful and appropriate clothes, not drawing undue attention to our bodies, or trying to fit in with the latest trends. It means thinking carefully about what we wear and why we wear it—are we trying to honor God or seek approval from the world? Modesty reflects a heart that is content in Christ and secure in His love rather than relying on outward appearance to find our value.

However, modesty is not just about what we wear—it extends to every part of our behavior. How we speak, treat others, and carry ourselves reflects whether we live a life that honors God. Proverbs 31:25 speaks of the virtuous woman, saying, "Strength and honour are her clothing; and she shall rejoice in time to come." A modest woman is mindful of her physical appearance and seeks to live with integrity, respect, and humility in all areas of her life. This means speaking with kindness and grace, treating others with respect, and carrying ourselves with dignity, no matter the situation. Modesty in behavior is about living in a way that points others to Christ rather than drawing attention to ourselves.

Modesty in appearance and behavior also involves having a heart of humility. Philippians 2:3-4 reminds us, "Let nothing be done through strife or vainglory; but in lowliness of mind let each esteem other better than themselves. Look not every man on his own things, but every man also on the things of others." Modesty means putting others before ourselves and not seeking to elevate or impress others for personal gain. Whether through our clothing choices, actions, or words, modesty involves considering how our behavior affects those around us and ensuring that we act in a way that reflects Christ's love and humility.

In addition to clothing and behavior, modesty is about self-control in all aspects of life. Titus 2:11-12 teaches us, "For the grace of God that bringeth salvation hath appeared to all men, teaching us that, denying ungodliness and worldly lusts, we should live soberly, righteously, and godly, in this present world." Modesty involves saying no to the things of the world that would lead us away from God's standards, whether in the way we dress, talk, or act. It means having the self-discipline to avoid behaviors and choices that do not align with God's Word and instead choosing to live righteously and godly, even in a world that often promotes the opposite.

Modesty also reflects a desire to honor God in all that we do. Colossians 3:17 reminds us, "And whatsoever ye do in word or deed, do all in the name of the Lord Jesus, giving thanks to God and the Father by him." Whether through our appearance, actions, or relationships, we are called to live in a way that honors God and points others to Him. Modesty is not about following rules—it's about having a heart that desires to please God in every aspect of life. When we choose to honor God, whether through how we dress, speak, or treat others, we live out the true meaning of modesty.

It's also important to remember that modesty reflects our identity in Christ. As believers, our value and worth come from who we are in Christ, not from how we look or wear. Galatians 3:26-27 says, "For ye are all the children of God by faith in Christ Jesus. For as many of you as have been baptized into Christ have put on Christ." When we put on Christ, we are clothed in His righteousness, and our identity is found in Him alone. Modesty is about living in a way that reflects that identity, not seeking validation from the world or trying to gain approval through outward appearance. Our worth is found in Christ, and when we understand that, we can live with confidence and security, knowing that we are fully loved and accepted by God.

Modesty also helps protect us from the pressures and temptations of the world. Romans 12:2 warns, "And be not conformed to this world: but be ye transformed by the renewing of your mind, that ye may prove what is that good, and acceptable, and perfect, will of God." The world often promotes values that oppose God's standards, encouraging immodesty, selfishness, and pride. But as followers of Christ, we are called to be different, to live according to God's will, not the world's. Modesty is a way of standing apart from the world and choosing to live in a way that reflects God's truth. It helps us resist the temptation to conform to the world's standards and instead live in a pleasing way to God.

In conclusion, modesty in appearance and behavior is about much more than just clothing—it reflects a heart that seeks to honor God in every aspect of life. 1 Timothy 2:9 and 1 Peter 3:3-4 remind us that true beauty and worth come not from outward appearance but from the hidden man of the heart. Modesty involves making choices that reflect humility, respect, and self-control in how we dress and conduct ourselves. It means living to honor God in all we do, putting others before ourselves, and resisting the world's pressures. As believers, our identity is found in Christ, and when we understand that, we can live confidently, knowing that we are fully loved and accepted by Him. Let us strive to live modestly, not just in our appearance but in our actions and attitudes, as a reflection of our desire to honor God and to live according to His Word.

Chapter 5 - Magnify the Lord

To magnify the Lord is one of the most essential principles for anyone who desires to live a life that honors God. The idea of magnifying the Lord is not about making God bigger than He already is—He is infinitely great and glorious—but about making His greatness more visible through our lives. Just as a magnifying glass brings something into more precise focus or makes small details more noticeable, magnifying the Lord means bringing attention to God's glory, goodness, and power in everything we do. It means that our lives reflect His praise, and we live in such a way that others can see His love, grace, and presence through us. Psalm 34:3 says, "O magnify the Lord with me, and let us exalt his name together." This verse invites us to make our lives a continual act of worship, to join others in praising God, and to give Him glory in all things, big and small. It reminds us that our purpose is to lift God's name, to exalt Him above all else, and to live in a way that directs others toward His greatness.

Magnifying the Lord isn't just something we do in moments of worship or prayer; it's a way of life. Philippians 1:20 provides a powerful example of this when the apostle Paul says, "Christ shall be magnified in my body, whether it be by life, or by death." Paul's statement reveals that magnifying the Lord is about glorifying God in every circumstance, whether in times of joy or suffering, life or even death. It means that no matter what we are going through, we give God the glory and trust that He is at work in every situation. To magnify the Lord in our lives means that everything we do—our words, actions, choices, and struggles—should point back to God and reflect His glory. It is about making sure that our lives are centered on Him, that we are living for His purpose, and that we are continually showing others who He is through how we live.

Living a life that magnifies the Lord requires a heart that is fully surrendered to Him. When we magnify God, we acknowledge He is greater than anything else in our lives—more splendid than our desires, plans, and understanding. Proverbs 3:5 - 6 reminds us to "Trust in the Lord with all thine heart; and lean not unto thine own understanding. In all thy ways acknowledge him, and he shall direct thy paths." Trusting God and acknowledging Him in all we do is crucial to magnifying the Lord. It means putting God first in every decision, seeking His guidance, and trusting His plan is better than our own. When we live with this kind of trust and surrender, we bring glory to God because we show the world that He is worthy of our trust and that His ways are perfect.

To magnify the Lord also means living with gratitude and praise. Psalm 100:4 encourages us to "Enter into his gates with thanksgiving, and into his courts with praise: be thankful unto him, and bless his name." A thankful heart magnifies the Lord because it acknowledges His goodness and recognizes that every blessing comes from Him. When we focus on God's goodness, even in difficult times, we magnify Him by showing that our hope and joy come from Him, not our circumstances. Gratitude shifts our perspective and helps us see God's hand in our lives, even when things are tough. Living with a heart of praise and thanksgiving makes God's greatness more visible to others and invites them to see His goodness through our lives.

Magnifying the Lord also involves how we treat others. Jesus taught us to love our neighbors as ourselves and to reflect His love to the world. In Matthew 5:16, Jesus says, "Let your light so shine before men, that they may see your good works, and glorify your Father which is in heaven." When we love others, serve them, and treat them with kindness and compassion, we magnify the Lord because we show His love in action. Our good works are not about bringing attention to ourselves but pointing others to God and giving Him the glory. When people see the love of Christ in us, they are drawn to God, and our lives reflect His love and grace.

Another vital aspect of magnifying the Lord is obeying His Word. John 14:15 says, "If ye love me, keep my commandments." Obeying God's commandments shows our love for Him and magnifies His authority. When we choose to follow God's Word, even when it's difficult or goes against the grain of society, we demonstrate that His ways are higher than ours and that we trust His wisdom. Obedience brings glory to God because it shows that we live according to His truth and not the world's standards. Through our obedience, others can see Christ's difference in our lives and are drawn to Him.

Magnifying the Lord also means sharing the gospel and telling others about what God has done in our lives. Psalm 105:1 says, "O give thanks unto the Lord; call upon his name: make known his deeds among the people." Sharing our testimony and telling others how God has worked in our lives is a powerful way to magnify Him. When we speak about God's faithfulness, mercy, and grace, we give Him the glory and help others to see His greatness. Through our words and actions, we can point others to Christ and invite them to experience His love and salvation.

Magnifying the Lord isn't something that only happens in the good times; we are called to do it even in trials and suffering. James 1:2-3 tells us, "My brethren, count it all joy when ye fall into divers temptations; Knowing this, that the trying of your faith worketh patience." One of the most potent ways to magnify Him is to praise God and give Him glory, even when we are going through difficult times. It shows that our faith is not dependent on our circumstances but on the unchanging character of God. When we continue to trust and praise Him during trials, we demonstrate to the world that He is worthy of our worship, no matter what. Our faithfulness under challenging times magnifies God's strength and faithfulness, showing others He is our refuge and help.

Another way to magnify the Lord is by living with integrity and honesty. Proverbs 11:3 says, "The integrity of the upright shall guide them." Living a life of integrity, where our words and actions align with God's truth, brings glory to God because it shows that we are committed to living according to His standards. When honest, trustworthy, and faithful in our relationships and responsibilities, we reflect God's character and show the world what it means to live a life that honors Him. Integrity is a powerful testimony to the transforming work of Christ in our lives, and it magnifies God's goodness and righteousness.

In addition to how we live our daily lives, we can magnify the Lord through our worship. Worship is more than just singing songs on Sunday—it's a lifestyle of giving God the honor and praise He deserves. Psalm 29:2 encourages us to "Give unto the Lord the glory due unto his name; worship the Lord in the beauty of holiness." Worshiping God means recognizing His greatness and lifting His name in praise. It's about setting aside time each day to focus on Him, to thank Him for His blessings, and to acknowledge His sovereignty in our lives. When we worship, we magnify God by declaring His worth and giving Him the glory for all He has done.

Magnifying the Lord also means trusting Him in every aspect of our lives. Proverbs 3:5-6 reminds us, "Trust in the Lord with all thine heart; and lean not unto thine own understanding. In all thy ways acknowledge him, and he shall direct thy paths." Trusting God and acknowledging Him in all we do is crucial to magnifying the Lord. It means relying on His wisdom rather than our own and seeking His guidance in every decision. When we trust God, we give Him the glory because we show that we believe in His goodness and faithfulness. Trusting God in life's big and small decisions magnifies His role as our guide and protector.

In conclusion, magnifying the Lord is about living a life that reflects praise to God in everything we do. Psalm 34:3 invites us to "magnify the Lord" and "exalt his name together," reminding us that our lives should be a continual act of worship, lifting God's name in all things. Philippians 1:20 challenges us to magnify Christ, whether in life or death, showing that our purpose is to glorify God no matter the circumstances. To magnify the Lord means to live with a heart of gratitude and praise, to treat others with love and kindness, to obey God's commandments, to share the gospel, and to trust Him in every aspect of our lives. It's about living with integrity, worshiping God with all our hearts, and giving Him glory in both good and bad. As we magnify the Lord daily, we point others to His greatness and make His glory more visible. Let us commit to magnifying the Lord in all we do so that our lives reflect His love, grace, and power, and others will be drawn to Him through our example.

Chapter 6 - Meekness in Spirit

Meekness in Spirit is one of the most misunderstood yet compelling qualities that God values. Often, meekness is mistaken for weakness, but in reality, meekness is strength under control. It is the ability to remain calm, humble, and patient in the face of challenges, trusting that God is in control and that His timing is perfect. Meekness reflects a quiet strength that doesn't rely on boasting or aggression to assert itself but instead rests in the assurance of God's sovereignty. This kind of spirit is precious in the eyes of God because it demonstrates trust, humility, and faith in His power rather than our own.

Matthew 5:5, one of the Beatitudes in Jesus' Sermon on the Mount, tells us, "Blessed are the meek: for they shall inherit the earth." This verse shows how highly God values meekness and gives us a promise that God will reward those who cultivate meekness in their hearts. To inherit the earth means to receive God's blessings, not necessarily in material wealth, but in the sense of receiving His favor, peace, and eternal inheritance. In a world where many seek to dominate or control through power, aggression, or pride, God flips the script by promising blessings to those who demonstrate meekness, showing that true greatness comes not from self-exaltation but from trusting in Him.

Meekness is also an essential aspect of how we interact with others. 1 Peter 3:4 emphasizes the importance of a "meek and quiet spirit," calling it an "ornament" of great value in God's sight. An ornament is something that is cherished, something that enhances and beautifies, and in this context, a meek spirit is described as an adornment that makes us truly beautiful in God's eyes. It's not about outward appearance or trying to impress others but about the inner beauty of the heart. A meek spirit is quiet, not in the sense of silence, but in calmness, gentleness, and a peaceful demeanor. This kind of spirit reflects inner strength and confidence from trusting God fully.

One of the critical characteristics of meekness is its reliance on God's timing. So often in life, we want things to happen quickly, and we may feel tempted to take matters into our own hands when things don't go according to our plans. However, meekness teaches us to be patient and to trust that God's timing is perfect. Proverbs 3:5-6 reminds us to "Trust in the Lord with all thine heart; and lean not unto thine own understanding. In all thy ways acknowledge him, and he shall direct thy paths." Meekness is rooted in this kind of trust. It's the understanding that we don't need to force our way or rush ahead because God is in control and will direct our steps in His perfect time. This quiet confidence allows us to wait on God and rest in His promises, knowing He is faithful.

Meekness is also about humility, a willingness to put others before ourselves and to serve without seeking recognition. Philippians 2:3-4 teaches us, "Let nothing be done through strife or vainglory; but in lowliness of mind let each esteem other better than themselves. Look not every man on his own things, but every man also on the things of others." A meek spirit does not seek attention or praise but aims to serve others in love and humility. This kind of humility is not about thinking less of ourselves but of ourselves less. It's about recognizing that we are here to serve and to love others just as Christ served and loved us.

Jesus Himself is the ultimate example of meekness. In Matthew 11:29, Jesus invites us to "Take my yoke upon you, and learn of me; for I am meek and lowly in heart: and ye shall find rest unto your souls." With all power and authority, Jesus, the Son of God, chose to live in meekness and humility. He did not come to earth to dominate or force His way upon people; instead, He came as a servant, showing love, compassion, and patience to those who needed Him. His life was marked by meekness, and He calls us to follow His example. Meekness doesn't mean being passive or weak—it means trusting God's strength rather than relying on our own and choosing to love and serve others instead of seeking our gain.

Meekness also plays a significant role in responding to conflict and adversity. When we face challenges or criticism, it can be easy to react with anger, defensiveness, or pride. But meekness calls us to respond with gentleness and patience. James 1:19-20 says, "Wherefore, my beloved brethren, let every man be swift to hear, slow to speak, slow to wrath: For the wrath of man worketh not the righteousness of God." A meek spirit is slow to anger, choosing to listen, understand, and respond with grace instead. This doesn't mean that we allow others to walk all over us or avoid standing up for what is right, but it does mean that we handle situations with gentleness and self-control, trusting that God will work things out in His time.

One of the most potent aspects of meekness is its ability to reflect God's character. When we live with a meek spirit, we are showing others what it looks like to trust in God's sovereignty and to live with quiet strength. 2 Corinthians

12:9-10 reminds us of the power that comes from recognizing our weakness and relying on God's strength: "And he said unto me, My grace is sufficient for thee: for my strength is made perfect in weakness. Most gladly therefore will I rather glory in my infirmities, that the power of Christ may rest upon me." Meekness is not about being strong in our power but finding strength in our dependence on God. Through our meekness, others can see Christ's power at work in us, as we live not by our strength but by the strength that comes from the Holy Spirit.

Meekness also allows us to receive correction and instruction with a humble heart. Proverbs 9:9 says, "Give instruction to a wise man, and he will be yet wiser: teach a just man, and he will increase in learning." A meek spirit is willing to learn, to admit when we are wrong, and to grow from the wisdom and guidance of others. Pride resists correction, but meekness welcomes it, knowing that it helps us to grow closer to God and to become more like Christ. This willingness to learn and develop is vital to living a pleasing life to God.

In relationships, meekness creates peace and harmony. Ephesians 4:2 encourages us to live "with all lowliness and meekness, with longsuffering, forbearing one another in love." A meek spirit is patient and kind, willing to bear with others in love even when they are difficult or frustrating. It seeks to maintain unity and peace rather than stirring up conflict or division. In a world that often values assertiveness and self-promotion, meekness offers a refreshing alternative that values humility, patience, and love. When we live with meekness, we reflect Christ's love and create an environment of peace and grace in our relationships.

Another essential aspect of meekness is its connection to contentment. Philippians 4:11-12 teaches us, "Not that I speak in respect of want: for I have learned, in whatsoever state I am, therewith to be content." A meek spirit is content in all circumstances, trusting that God knows what is best and that He will provide for our needs. Meekness doesn't seek wealth, status, or power but instead finds peace and joy in trusting God's provision and plan. This contentment is a powerful testimony to the world because it shows that our hope and security are not found in material things but in our relationship with God.

In conclusion, meekness in spirit is a quality that God highly values because it reflects strength under control, humility, and trust in His sovereignty. Matthew 5:5 promises that the meek will inherit the earth, showing that God blesses those who live with a spirit of humility and trust in Him. 1 Peter 3:4 reminds us that a meek and quiet spirit is of great value in God's sight, emphasizing that it is the inner beauty of the heart that matters most to God. Meekness is not about being weak or passive—it is about trusting in God's strength, living with humility, and choosing to serve others in love. It means responding to conflict with gentleness, receiving correction with a humble heart, and finding contentment in God's provision. Jesus Himself is the perfect example of meekness, and He calls us to follow His example by living with a meek spirit that reflects His love and grace to the world. As we cultivate meekness in our lives, we can trust that God will bless us, guide us, and use us to bring glory to His name.

Chapter 7 - Mercy Toward Others

Mercy toward others is one of the most essential and beautiful qualities we are called to live out as Christians. It reflects the heart of God, who has shown us incredible mercy and kindness through Jesus Christ. To show mercy means to extend forgiveness, compassion, and understanding to others, even when they don't deserve it, just as God has done for us. Mercy is a form of love that is patient, kind, and willing to overlook offenses. It's not always easy to be merciful, especially when we feel hurt or wronged by someone, but the Bible teaches us that mercy is a quality that brings blessing and is highly valued by God. Matthew 5:7 says, "Blessed are the merciful: for they shall obtain mercy." This verse is part of the Beatitudes in Jesus' Sermon on the Mount, where He describes the attitudes and behaviors that God blesses. Those who show mercy will receive mercy in return, not only from others but from God Himself. The act of showing mercy reflects our understanding and appreciation of the mercy that God has shown us.

Mercy is central to the character of God. The Bible shows examples of God's mercy toward His people, even when they fail Him. In the Old Testament, we read about how the Israelites repeatedly turned away from God, yet He continued to show them mercy, offering forgiveness and a way back to Him. Lamentations 3:22-23 says, "It is of the Lord's mercies that we are not consumed, because his compassions fail not. They are new every morning: great is thy faithfulness." This verse reminds us that God's mercies are constant and never-ending. Every day, He offers us new mercies, forgiving our sins and inviting us to draw closer to Him. Just as God has shown us mercy, we are called to show mercy to others. When we extend mercy, we reflect God's love and grace to the world around us.

Ephesians 4:32 teaches us, "And be ye kind one to another, tenderhearted, forgiving one another, even as God for Christ's sake hath forgiven you." This verse beautifully sums up the Christian call to show mercy and kindness to others. We are to be tenderhearted, which means having compassion and empathy for the people around us, recognizing their struggles, and choosing to respond with love instead of judgment. Forgiveness is a critical part of mercy. Just as God has forgiven us through Christ, we are called to forgive those who wrong us. This doesn't mean that the hurt or pain we've experienced isn't authentic or significant, but it means letting go of bitterness and resentment offering grace and forgiveness in the same way God has done for us. Forgiveness is one of the highest forms of mercy because it allows healing and restoration in our hearts and relationships.

Mercy isn't just about forgiveness—it also involves showing kindness and compassion to those in need. In the parable of the Good Samaritan (Luke 10:30-37), Jesus tells the story of a man who was beaten and left for dead by the side of the road. Several people passed by without helping, but a Samaritan considered an outsider and unlikely to help, stopped and showed mercy to the injured man. He bandaged the man's wounds, took him to an inn, and cared for him. Jesus used this story to illustrate what it means to love our neighbors and show mercy, even to those we might consider different. Mercy goes beyond just feeling sympathy for someone's suffering—it leads to action. It's about stepping in to help those in need through physical assistance, emotional support, or simply being present for someone hurting. When we show mercy, we are living out the love of Christ and demonstrating that everyone is valuable and deserving of compassion.

Showing mercy also means being slow to anger and quick to forgive. James 1:19 instructs us, "Wherefore, my beloved brethren, let every man be swift to hear, slow to speak, slow to wrath." When we are merciful, we don't rush to judge or react angrily when someone wrongs us. Instead, we take the time to listen, to understand their perspective, and to respond with kindness. Mercy doesn't mean ignoring wrongdoing or pretending that everything is okay, but it means choosing to react in a way that seeks reconciliation rather than revenge. Proverbs 19:11 says, "The discretion of a man deferreth his anger; and it is his glory to pass over a transgression." When we show mercy by letting go of anger and choosing not to hold grudges, we reflect God's heart of forgiveness and grace.

One of the most profound ways to show mercy is by praying for those who have hurt us. In Matthew 5:44, Jesus tells us, "But I say unto you, Love your enemies, bless them that curse you, do good to them that hate you, and pray for them which despitefully use you, and persecute you." This is perhaps one of the most challenging aspects of mercy because it goes against our natural inclination to seek justice or revenge. But when we pray for those who have wronged us, we ask God to work in their hearts and bring healing and restoration for them and us. Prayer helps to soften our hearts toward those who have hurt us and allows God to work in ways we might not be able to see. It's an act of surrender, trusting that God's justice and mercy are more significant than our own and that He can bring true healing and reconciliation.

Mercy is not just something we show to others—it's something we receive from God daily. None of us are perfect, and we all fall short of God's standards. Romans 3:23 reminds us, "For all have sinned, and come short of the glory of God." But in His great love for us, God offers us mercy through Jesus Christ. Romans 5:8 says, "But God commendeth his love toward us, in that, while we were yet sinners, Christ died for us." Jesus' sacrifice on the cross is the ultimate act of mercy, offering us forgiveness and salvation when we didn't deserve it. Understanding the depth of God's mercy toward us should inspire us to show that same mercy to others. When we realize how much we have been forgiven, it becomes easier to forgive those who wrong us and to extend kindness and compassion to those in need.

Living a life of mercy also involves seeing people how God sees them. Often, we are quick to judge others based on their actions, appearances, or circumstances. But mercy requires us to look beyond the surface and to see people as valuable and loved by God. Jesus demonstrated this kind of mercy throughout His ministry, particularly in how He treated those marginalized or looked down upon by society. Whether it was the woman caught in adultery (John 8:1-11), the tax collector Zacchaeus (Luke 19:1-10), or the lepers who were considered unclean (Luke 17:11-19), Jesus consistently showed mercy to those who were rejected by others. He didn't condemn or cast them aside—instead, He offered them love, healing, and forgiveness. As followers of Christ, we are called to do the same. We are called to show mercy to everyone, regardless of background, mistakes, or status, because everyone is made in God's image.

Showing mercy can sometimes be difficult, especially when someone doesn't deserve it. But mercy is not about what someone deserves—it's about reflecting the grace and love that God has shown us. Micah 6:8 reminds us, "He hath shewed thee, O man, what is good; and what doth the Lord require of thee, but to do justly, and to love mercy, and to walk humbly with thy God?" Mercy is not just an option for Christians—it is something God requires of us. We must live out our faith and walk in humility before God. When we show mercy, we demonstrate that we understand the depth of God's mercy toward us and are willing to extend that same grace to others.

Mercy also brings healing to the person who shows it and receives it. Proverbs 11:17 says, "The merciful man doeth good to his own soul: but he that is cruel troubleth his own flesh." When we show mercy, it brings peace to our hearts and frees us from bitterness and resentment. Mercy allows us to move forward with love and compassion rather than being weighed down by anger or unforgiveness. It also has the power to bring healing to broken relationships. When we choose to forgive and show mercy, we open the door for reconciliation and restoration, allowing God's love to mend what was broken.

In conclusion, mercy toward others is a central part of living a life that reflects God's love and grace. Matthew 5:7 promises that those who are merciful will receive mercy, and Ephesians 4:32 calls us to be kind, tenderhearted, and forgiving, just as God has forgiven us through Christ. Mercy involves forgiveness, compassion, and kindness, even when brutal or undeserved. It's about responding to others with love instead of judgment and taking action to help those in need. Mercy reflects the heart of God, who has shown us incredible mercy through Jesus Christ, offering us forgiveness and salvation when we didn't deserve it. As we receive God's mercy, we are called to extend that same mercy to others, recognizing that everyone is valuable and loved by God. By living a life of mercy, we are not only reflecting God's character to the world but also experiencing the peace, healing, and blessings that come from following His example. Let us strive to be people who show mercy, just as God has shown mercy to us, and let our lives reflect His love, grace, and forgiveness.

Chapter 8 - Manage Your Time Wisely

Managing your time wisely is one of the most important lessons for anyone, especially young people seeking to live a life that honors God. Time is a precious gift from the Lord, and how we use it reflects what we value most. The Bible teaches us to be mindful of how we spend our time, focusing on things with eternal significance rather than getting caught up in distractions that can pull us away from God's purpose for our lives. In Ephesians 5:16, the apostle Paul reminds us to "redeem the time, because the days are evil." This verse emphasizes the urgency of making the most of every moment, recognizing that we live in a world where time can easily slip away and opportunities to serve the Lord and make an impact can be lost if we are not intentional. Redeeming time means using it wisely, not wasting it on things that don't matter in the long run, and making choices that align with God's will for our lives.

Colossians 4:5 echoes this message, telling us to "walk in wisdom toward them that are without, redeeming the time." This means we should live wisely, especially how we interact with those around us. Our time is not just for ourselves—it's also for serving others and sharing God's love and truth with them. Time spent loving others, encouraging them, and sharing the gospel is time invested in eternity. When we manage our time wisely, we prioritize what is most important, seeking to use every opportunity to live for the Lord and to make a difference in the lives of others. This doesn't mean that we need to be constantly busy or that we can never rest, but it does mean that we should be intentional about how we spend our time, making sure that we are using it for God's glory.

One of the most significant challenges today is the sheer number of distractions that can take up our time. With social media, entertainment, and endless forms of communication, it's easy to lose hours of our day without even realizing it. While these things aren't necessarily bad in and of themselves, they can become time-wasters if we aren't careful. That's why it's important to regularly evaluate how we spend our time and whether or not our activities are helping us grow in our relationship with God or pulling us away from Him. Psalm 90:12 says, "So teach us to number our days, that we may apply our hearts unto wisdom." This verse reminds us that our time on earth is limited, and we should live with the awareness that every day is a gift from God. We should seek

His wisdom in how we spend each day, focusing on things that will have lasting value.

Living with purpose means setting priorities based on what matters most to God. Matthew 6:33 instructs us, "But seek ye first the kingdom of God, and his righteousness; and all these things shall be added unto you." When we prioritize seeking God's kingdom, everything else falls into place. This doesn't mean we should neglect our daily responsibilities, but it does mean that our priority should always be our relationship with God and His plan for our lives. When we make time for prayer, Bible study, worship, and serving others, we invest in things with eternal value. These activities help us grow closer to God and strengthen our faith, preparing us to face whatever challenges life may bring.

Managing our time wisely also recognizes that not every opportunity comes from God. Sometimes, we may feel overwhelmed by the number of things we are asked to do or the expectations placed on us by others. While it's essential to serve and help others, it's also important to seek God's guidance in deciding which activities to pursue. Ecclesiastes 3:1 reminds us, "To every thing there is a season, and a time to every purpose under the heaven." God has a perfect timing for everything, and part of managing our time wisely is learning to discern when it's time to say yes and when it's time to say no. We can't do everything, and we shouldn't try to. Instead, we should seek God's wisdom in choosing how to spend our time so that we can focus on what He has called us to do in each season of life.

For young people, the temptation to waste time can be powerful. It's easy to think that we have plenty of time ahead of us and can always get serious about our faith or goals later. But the Bible encourages us not to waste our youth but to live purposefully for the Lord. In 1 Timothy 4:12, Paul tells Timothy, "Let no man despise thy youth; but be thou an example of the believers, in word, in conversation, in charity, in spirit, in faith, in purity." This verse reminds young people that they have an essential role in God's kingdom and don't have to wait until they are older to start living for the Lord. Every day is an opportunity to serve God, to grow in faith, and to make an impact for His glory. Whether studying the Bible, serving in your church, helping others, or simply living a life that reflects Christ's love, young people can redeem time by focusing on things with eternal significance.

Another critical aspect of managing our time wisely is balancing work and rest. God created us to work, but He also made us to rest. In Exodus 20:8-10, God commands us to remember the Sabbath day and to keep it holy, setting aside time for rest and worship. Rest is a vital part of living a balanced life, and when we take time to rest, we trust that God will take care of the things we can't. Resting doesn't mean being lazy or avoiding responsibility but taking time to recharge, reflect, and refocus on God. Jesus Himself often took time to rest and pray, even in His busy ministry. Mark 6:31 tells us that Jesus told His disciples, "Come ye yourselves apart into a desert place, and rest a while." If Jesus needed time to rest, then we certainly do too. When we manage our time wisely, we ensure time for work and rest, trusting that God will give us the strength and wisdom we need daily.

In addition to balancing work and rest, managing our time wisely also means being good stewards of the opportunities God gives us. In the parable of the talents (Matthew 25:14-30), Jesus tells the story of a master who entrusts his servants with different amounts of money (called talents) and expects them to invest it wisely. The servants who use their abilities to produce more are praised and rewarded, while those who bury their talent out of fear are rebuked. This parable teaches us the importance of using the gifts, abilities, and opportunities God gives us for His glory. Whether it's our time, talents, or resources, we are called to be good stewards, using what God has given us to serve Him and others. When we manage our time wisely, we make the most of God's opportunities, whether in our work, relationships, or ministry.

Managing our time wisely also involves setting goals and making plans. Proverbs 21:5 says, "The thoughts of the diligent tend only to plenteousness; but of every one that is hasty only to want." This verse reminds us that planning and diligence lead to success while rushing into things without careful thought often leads to failure. Setting goals helps us stay focused on what's essential and ensures that we use our time in a way that aligns with God's purposes for our lives. However, while making plans is vital, we must also be flexible and open to God's leadership. Proverbs 16:9 says, "A man's heart deviseth his way: but the Lord directeth his steps." We can make plans, but we must always be willing to adjust those plans if God leads us in a different direction. Part of managing our time wisely is being sensitive to the Holy Spirit's guidance and being willing to follow God's plan, even if it's different from our own.

Finally, managing our time wisely means living with an eternal perspective. Colossians 3:2 instructs us, "Set your affection on things above, not on things on the earth." When we focus on things that have eternal value, we are less likely to waste time on things that don't matter. This doesn't mean that we can't enjoy hobbies, entertainment, or time with friends and family, but it does mean that we should always keep our ultimate purpose in mind: to glorify God and to live for His kingdom. Every day is an opportunity to invest in things that have eternal significance—whether through sharing the gospel, encouraging someone in their faith, helping those in need, or simply living a life that reflects Christ's love and grace.

In conclusion, managing your time wisely is about making the most of every moment, focusing on things that have eternal value, and living with purpose for the Lord. Ephesians 5:16 and Colossians 4:5 remind us to redeem the time because the days are evil, urging us to use our time for God's glory and to impact His kingdom. Managing our time wisely involves setting priorities, seeking God's wisdom, and being intentional about how we spend each day. It means avoiding distractions, balancing work and rest, being good stewards of God's opportunities, and living with an eternal perspective. Time is a precious gift; when we use it wisely, we honor God and live out His purpose. Let us strive to manage our time in a way that reflects our love for the Lord and our desire to serve Him, making every moment count for His glory.

Chapter 9 - Mind Your Words

The power of words cannot be underestimated, as they can either uplift or tear down, encourage or discourage, speak life or cause harm. In the Bible, God teaches us the importance of choosing words wisely and understanding that what we say can profoundly impact ourselves and others. The verse Proverbs 18:21 says, "Death and life are in the power of the tongue," highlighting the incredible influence our speech has on the world around us. Every word we speak carries weight, whether we realize it or not. Words can bring healing, comfort, and truth or spread negativity, hurt, and division. As Christians, we must be mindful of how we use this powerful gift of language. We are urged to speak life—words that build up, encourage and bring hope to others—while avoiding gossip, slander, and harshness that can cause pain or misunderstanding.

Ephesians 4:29 also emphasizes this, instructing, "Let no corrupt communication proceed out of your mouth, but that which is good to the use of edifying, that it may minister grace unto the hearers." This verse provides clear guidance on how we should communicate with others. Our words should be pure, uplifting, and gracious. We are to avoid corrupt or harmful speech, choosing to speak in ways that help and encourage those around us. The word "edifying" means to build up, and this is the purpose of our speech as followers of Christ: to build up others in love, truth, and kindness. When mindful of our words, we can positively impact those we encounter, offering encouragement and hope in a world that often promotes negativity and criticism.

One of the critical aspects of minding our words is understanding that what we say reflects what is in our hearts. Luke 6:45 tells us, "A good man out of the good treasure of his heart bringeth forth that which is good; and an evil man out of the evil treasure of his heart bringeth forth that which is evil: for of the abundance of the heart his mouth speaketh." Our words are a direct reflection of what is happening inside us. If our hearts are filled with love, kindness, and the truth of God's Word, our speech will naturally reflect those qualities. But if our hearts are filled with bitterness, anger, or selfishness, that will also come through in our words. This is why it's so essential to guard not only our tongues but also our hearts. The more we fill our hearts with God's truth and love, the more our speech will reflect His character.

One of the most harmful ways we can misuse our words is through gossip and slander. Gossip involves talking about someone behind their back in a way that spreads negativity or false information, and it can cause tremendous damage to relationships and reputations. Proverbs 16:28 warns, "A froward man soweth strife: and a whisperer separateth chief friends." Gossip and slander can create division between even the closest friends, and they go against the call to love and support one another. As Christians, we are called to avoid gossip and speak words of truth and encouragement. When we are tempted to talk negatively about others, we should remember the words of James 1:19, which say, "Wherefore, my beloved brethren, let every man be swift to hear, slow to speak, slow to wrath." Being slow to speak means thinking carefully before we say anything, ensuring that our words will not cause harm or division.

Harsh words are another way we can misuse the power of our tongues. In moments of frustration or anger, it's easy to lash out with hurtful words that we may later regret. However, harsh words can leave lasting scars on others, damaging relationships and causing emotional pain. Proverbs 15:1 says, "A soft answer turneth away wrath: but grievous words stir up anger." This verse teaches us the value of responding gently and calmly, even under challenging situations. Harsh words only worsen conflict and worsen conditions, but a kind and gentle response can diffuse tension and bring peace. When we respond with grace rather than anger, we reflect the love of Christ and can bring healing instead of harm.

Minding our words also involves speaking the truth, even when it is difficult. Ephesians 4:15 says, "But speaking the truth in love, may grow up into him in all things, which is the head, even Christ." Speaking the truth is essential, but it must always be done in love. This means that we should not use the truth as a weapon to hurt or criticize others but as a way to guide, support, and encourage them. Sometimes, we must speak brutal truths to someone, whether offering correction, pointing out a mistake, or addressing a sensitive issue. In these moments, it's essential to approach the conversation with love and kindness, ensuring our goal is to help and uplift, not tear down. Speaking truth in love helps build stronger, healthier relationships and reflects God's grace and patience toward us.

Another important aspect of minding our words is the practice of encouragement. Encouraging others is one of the most powerful ways we can use our words to make a positive impact. Proverbs 12:25 says, "Heaviness in the heart of man maketh it stoop: but a good word maketh it glad." When someone feels discouraged, anxious, or weighed down by life's challenges, a simple word of encouragement can lift their spirits and bring hope. Whether offering a kind compliment, reminding someone of God's promises, or simply telling them that you are there for them, words of encouragement can bring light into the darkest situations. As followers of Christ, we are called to be a source of encouragement to others, using our words to build them up and point them to the hope we have in Jesus.

Prayer is another essential way we can use our words for good. James 5:16 encourages us to "pray one for another, that ye may be healed. The effectual fervent prayer of a righteous man availeth much." Prayer is a powerful tool, not only for strengthening our relationship with God but also for interceding on behalf of others. When we take the time to pray for those in need, whether for healing, guidance, or comfort, we use our words in a way that aligns with God's will and invites His power to work in the lives of those we are praying for. Prayer is one of the most loving and compassionate ways we can use our words, and it brings about real change and healing.

In addition to prayer, sharing the gospel is one of the most important ways we can use our words to speak life. Romans 10:14 asks, "How then shall they call on him in whom they have not believed? And how shall they believe in him of whom they have not heard? And how shall they hear without a preacher?" Sharing the good news of Jesus Christ with others is a way to offer them the greatest gift of all—eternal life. Our words can point others to the hope and salvation found in Jesus, which is one of the most important ways we can use the power of our tongues. Whether through a conversation with a friend, a kind word to a stranger, or a testimony shared in church, speaking about the love and grace of Jesus can change lives and bring people closer to God.

Our words also have the power to bring healing and reconciliation in broken relationships. Proverbs 12:18 says, "There is that speaketh like the piercings of a sword: but the tongue of the wise is health." Words can cut deeply, like a sword, causing pain and division, but they can also bring healing when spoken with wisdom and love. When conflicts arise in our relationships, choosing our words carefully and speaking with humility and grace can help restore peace and bring about reconciliation. Apologizing when we've said something hurtful, offering forgiveness, and speaking words of love and kindness can mend broken relationships and bring healing to both parties.

Being mindful of our words also means practicing self-control. James 3:8-10 describes the tongue as "an unruly evil, full of deadly poison" and warns that "therewith bless we God, even the Father; and therewith curse we men, which are made after the similitude of God." These verses remind us that while the tongue is small, it can cause great harm if not controlled. As Christians, we are called to exercise self-control in all areas of life, including our speech. This means thinking before we speak, being mindful of how our words will affect others, and choosing to communicate in ways that reflect God's love and truth. Self-control in our speech helps us avoid saying things we may later regret and ensures that our words are used for good.

In conclusion, minding your words is about recognizing the incredible power of the tongue and choosing to use it in a way that honors God and reflects His love. Proverbs 18:21 teaches us that "death and life are in the power of the tongue," reminding us that our words can either build up or tear down, heal, or harm. Ephesians 4:29 encourages us to let no corrupt communication come out of our mouths, but only that suitable for building up others. By choosing to speak life, encouragement, and truth, we can positively impact the people around us. Avoiding gossip, slander, and harsh words helps prevent unnecessary hurt and division while speaking words of love, kindness, and encouragement brings healing and hope. Our words reflect what's in our hearts, and when we fill our hearts with God's love and truth, our speech will naturally reflect His character. Whether through prayer, sharing the gospel, or simply offering a kind word to someone in need, we can use our words to point others to Jesus and bring healing and reconciliation to our relationships. Let us strive to be mindful of our words, using them to speak life, truth, and love and to bring glory to God in all we say.

Chapter 10 - Model Christ's Love

To model Christ's love is one of the most important and influential ways a Christian can live out their faith. The Bible calls us an example of Christ's love in everything we do, showing kindness, compassion, and selflessness to others, just as Jesus has shown us. In John 13:34-35, Jesus gives a new commandment to His disciples: "A new commandment I give unto you, That ye love one another; as I have loved you, that ye also love one another. By this shall all men know that ye are my disciples, if ye have love one to another." This is not just a suggestion but a command from Christ Himself, and it reveals that our love for one another is the defining characteristic of being His followers. Jesus didn't just tell us to love—He showed us what true love looks like through His life, ministry, and, ultimately, His sacrifice on the cross. To love like Christ means to love selflessly, sacrificially, and unconditionally, even when it's difficult and even when the people we are called to love may not deserve it. It means putting others before ourselves and seeking their good, just as Christ did for us.

In modeling Christ's love, we reflect the heart of God, who is the source of all love. 1 John 4:7 tells us, "Beloved, let us love one another: for love is of God; and every one that loveth is born of God, and knoweth God." The love we are called to show doesn't come from our strength or ability but God Himself. He is the source of all love, and as we grow in our relationship with Him, His love flows through us and enables us to love others in ways we couldn't on our own. When we love others with Christ's love, we reveal God's character to the world and show what it means to be a follower of Jesus. This kind of love is not based on feelings or emotions—it is a choice to act in love, even when it's hard, and to show kindness and compassion even to those who may not treat us well.

One of the critical aspects of modeling Christ's love is selflessness. In a world that often promotes selfishness and self-interest, Christ's love stands in stark contrast. Philippians 2:3-4 reminds us, "Let nothing be done through strife or vainglory; but in lowliness of mind let each esteem other better than themselves. Look not every man on his own things, but every man also on the things of others." To love like Christ means to put others before ourselves, to serve without expecting anything in return, and to seek the good of others, even when it requires sacrifice on our part. Jesus modeled this perfectly during His time on earth. He didn't come to be served but to serve and give His life as a ransom for many (Mark 10:45). He washed His disciples' feet, healed the sick, and reached out to those who were marginalized and outcasts. His love was always focused on others; we are called to do the same as His followers.

Compassion is another essential element of Christ's love. Throughout the Gospels, Jesus moved with compassion for the people He encountered. Whether it was feeding the hungry, healing the sick, or comforting the grieving, Jesus' actions were motivated by a deep compassion for the suffering and needs of others. Matthew 9:36 says, "But when he saw the multitudes, he was moved with compassion on them, because they fainted, and were scattered abroad, as sheep having no shepherd." Compassion goes beyond feeling sympathy for someone—it moves us to action. When we see someone in need, modeling Christ's love means responding with kindness and care, whether through offering help, providing comfort, or simply being there to listen and offer support. Jesus' compassion was not limited to those who followed Him or believed in Him—He showed compassion to everyone, regardless of their background, status, or faith. As His followers, we are called to extend that same compassion to everyone we meet, showing the love of Christ through our actions.

Another critical aspect of modeling Christ's love is forgiveness. Jesus taught about forgiveness and demonstrated it most powerfully on the cross. As He was crucified, He prayed, "Father, forgive them; for they know not what they do" (Luke 23:34). Even in His moment of most significant suffering, Jesus forgave those hurting Him. Forgiveness is one of the most challenging aspects of love, but it is essential to model Christ's love. In Ephesians 4:32, we are instructed, "And be ye kind one to another, tenderhearted, forgiving one another, even as God for Christ's sake hath forgiven you." When we forgive others, we reflect the grace and mercy God has shown us. Forgiveness brings healing and reconciliation, both in our hearts and in our relationships with others. It frees us from bitterness and anger and allows us to move forward in love, just as Christ forgave us and calls us to forgive others.

Patience is another essential quality of Christ's love. 1 Corinthians 13:4-5 tells us, "Charity suffereth long, and is kind; charity envieth not; charity vaunteth not itself, is not puffed up, Doth not behave itself unseemly, seeketh not her own, is not easily provoked, thinketh no evil." Christ-like love is patient and kind, even when others may test our patience or when situations are difficult. Patience is about enduring with grace and gentleness, choosing to love and serve others even when it's inconvenient or frustrating. Jesus showed incredible patience throughout His ministry, especially with His disciples, who often struggled to understand His teachings or who made mistakes. He never gave up on them but continued teaching, guiding, and loving them, helping them grow in their faith. As followers of Christ, we are called to show that same patience with others, understanding that love sometimes requires enduring difficult situations or extending grace when others fall short.

Humility is another vital aspect of Christ's love. Jesus, though He was the Son of God, humbled Himself and became a servant to others. Philippians 2:5-8 says, "Let this mind be in you, which was also in Christ Jesus: Who, being in the form of God, thought it not robbery to be equal with God: But made himself of no reputation, and took upon him the form of a servant, and was made in the likeness of men: And being found in fashion as a man, he humbled himself, and became obedient unto death, even the death of the cross." Jesus' love was marked by humility, as He willingly laid down His life for others. To model Christ's love, we must also embrace humility, recognizing that love is not about seeking recognition or praise for ourselves but about serving others in quiet, selfless ways. Humility allows us to put others first and to love without expecting anything in return.

Another critical aspect of modeling Christ's love is loving our enemies. In Matthew 5:44, Jesus teaches, "But I say unto you, Love your enemies, bless them that curse you, do good to them that hate you, and pray for them which despitefully use you, and persecute you." This kind of love radically differs from what the world teaches but is at the heart of Christ's message. Jesus didn't just love those who loved Him—He loved those who rejected Him, betrayed Him, and crucified Him. He calls us to do the same, to love those who are kind to us and those who may treat us poorly or oppose us. This kind of love is only possible through the power of the Holy Spirit, as we rely on God's strength to love others in ways that go beyond our natural ability. Loving our enemies reflects the depth of Christ's love, which is unconditional and sacrificial, and it shows the world the transformative power of God's grace.

To model Christ's love also means being a peacemaker. In Matthew 5:9, Jesus says, "Blessed are the peacemakers: for they shall be called the children of God." Peacemaking is about bringing reconciliation, healing, and unity in situations of conflict or division. Jesus is the ultimate peacemaker, as He reconciled us to God through His sacrifice on the cross. As His followers, we are called to be agents of peace in the world, promoting unity and harmony in our relationships and communities. This means resolving conflicts with grace, seeking to understand others, and working to bring people together rather than causing division or strife. Peacemaking is an expression of Christ's love because it seeks the well-being of others and reflects God's desire for reconciliation and unity.

Another important aspect of modeling Christ's love is living with integrity. 1 John 3:18 says, "My little children, let us not love in word, neither in tongue; but in deed and in truth." Love is not just about what we say but what we do. Our actions should match our words, and we should strive to live in a way that reflects the truth of Christ's love in every aspect of our lives. Integrity means living honestly, faithfully, and consistently, even when no one is watching. It means keeping our promises, being trustworthy, and treating others respectfully and fairly. When we live with integrity, we model Christ's love by showing that our faith is genuine and that we are committed to following His example in our words and actions.

In conclusion, modeling Christ's love is about living a life reflecting the love, grace, and compassion that Jesus has shown us.

John 13:34-35 and 1 John 4:7 remind us that love is the defining characteristic of a follower of Christ, and we are called to love others in the same way He has loved us. This kind of love is selfless, sacrificial, and unconditional. It involves showing compassion, kindness, forgiveness, patience, humility, and integrity in all that we do. It means loving those who are easy to love and those who may oppose or hurt us. When we model Christ's love, we reveal God's heart to the world and point others to His grace's transformative power. Let us strive to be examples of Christ's love in everything we do, living in a way that brings glory to God and reflects His love to those around us.

Chapter 11 - Maintain a Grateful Heart

A grateful heart is essential for a Christian's spiritual growth and well-being. Gratitude keeps us focused on God's goodness, no matter what circumstances we face, reminding us that His blessings and love are constant. It is easy to be thankful when things are going well, but the Bible teaches us to give thanks in every situation, even in trials and challenges. In 1 Thessalonians 5:18, we are instructed, "In every thing give thanks: for this is the will of God in Christ Jesus concerning you." This verse clarifies that gratitude is not just a suggestion but God's will for us. He wants us to maintain an attitude of thanksgiving in all circumstances because it shifts our focus from our problems to His provision, from our struggles to His strength. A heart of gratitude helps us trust in God's sovereignty, knowing He is in control and working all things together for our good, even when we don't understand why certain things are happening.

Gratitude has a powerful effect on our spiritual life, helping us to grow closer to God. When we thank God for His blessings—big and small—it strengthens our relationship with Him. Psalm 100:4 encourages us to "Enter into his gates with thanksgiving, and into his courts with praise: be thankful unto him, and bless his name." Thanksgiving opens the door to a deeper connection with God, inviting us into His presence with a heart full of praise. It allows us to recognize His hand in our lives and to see how He has been faithful in providing for our needs, protecting us, and guiding us. Gratitude fosters a sense of trust in God's faithfulness, reminding us that no matter what we face, He is always with us, and He will never leave or forsake us.

Colossians 3:15 says, "And let the peace of God rule in your hearts... and be ye thankful." This verse shows the connection between gratitude and peace. When we choose to be thankful, even in difficult circumstances, we allow God's peace to rule in our hearts. Gratitude shifts our perspective from worry and anxiety to trust and peace. It helps us focus on what we have rather than what we lack and reminds us that God's grace is sufficient for every need. A grateful heart is peaceful because it rests in knowing that God is in control and His good plans for us. Even when life doesn't go as planned, gratitude helps us to find peace amid uncertainty, knowing that God is working behind the scenes for our good and His glory.

Maintaining a grateful heart also helps us to cultivate joy, even in difficult times. James 1:2-3 encourages us to "Count it all joy when ye fall into divers temptations; Knowing this, that the trying of your faith worketh patience." While it may seem counterintuitive to find joy in trials, gratitude helps us to see the bigger picture. It reminds us that God uses our challenges to strengthen our faith and develop perseverance. When we choose to be thankful in hardship, we acknowledge that God is at work, even when we can't see it. Gratitude allows us to find joy in the journey, trusting that God uses every experience— good and bad—to shape us into the people He has called us to be. It helps us to keep our eyes on the eternal rather than getting bogged down by temporary difficulties.

A heart of gratitude also changes the way we interact with others. When we are grateful for God's blessings, we are more likely to be generous and kind to those around us. Gratitude fosters a spirit of humility, recognizing that everything we have is a gift from God, and it motivates us to share those blessings with others. In Ephesians 5:20, we are instructed to be "Giving thanks always for all things unto God and the Father in the name of our Lord Jesus Christ." This continuous attitude of thanksgiving helps us to develop a heart of compassion for others, knowing that just as God has been generous and kind to us, we are called to be gracious and kind to others. Gratitude leads to acts of service, helping us to live out our faith by loving and serving others as Christ has loved and served us.

Gratitude also protects our hearts from bitterness and discontentment. When we focus on what we don't have or compare ourselves to others, it's easy to become frustrated, envious, or discontent. However, being thankful for what we have guards our hearts against these negative emotions. Philippians 4:6-7 teaches us, "Be careful for nothing; but in every thing by prayer and supplication with thanksgiving let your requests be made known unto God. And the peace of God, which passeth all understanding, shall keep your hearts and minds through Christ Jesus." Gratitude turns our attention away from what we think we're missing and reminds us of all God has provided. It helps us trust that God knows what we need and will provide for us in His perfect timing. When we are thankful, we are less likely to compare ourselves to others and more likely to find contentment in the blessings God has given us.

Maintaining a grateful heart also keeps us grounded in the truth of who God is. Psalm 107:1 reminds us, "O give thanks unto the Lord, for he is good: for his mercy endureth forever." Gratitude helps us to remember that God is good, even when life is hard. It reminds us that His love and mercy are everlasting, and nothing can separate us from His love. When we focus on God's goodness, we are reminded of His character—His faithfulness, compassion, and grace. Gratitude helps us see God's hand at work in our lives, even in the small things and strengthens our faith in His ability to carry us through difficult times. By giving thanks in every situation, we proclaim our trust in God's goodness and His ability to work all things together for our good.

In addition to strengthening our relationship with God, gratitude strengthens our relationships with others. Expressing gratitude to the people in our lives—our family, friends, or coworkers—fosters a sense of connection and appreciation. Gratitude helps us to recognize the contributions of others and to acknowledge the ways they have blessed us. In 1 Thessalonians 1:2, Paul writes, "We give thanks to God always for you all, making mention of you in our prayers." This verse shows the importance of expressing gratitude for the people God has placed in our lives. When we take the time to thank others for their kindness, support, or encouragement, it strengthens our relationships and builds a sense of community. Gratitude helps us focus on the positive aspects of our relationships rather than dwelling on frustrations or misunderstandings. It fosters a spirit of unity and peace, allowing us to build stronger, healthier relationships with those around us.

Gratitude also helps us to persevere through difficult seasons. Focusing on what's going wrong or feeling overwhelmed by our circumstances can be tempting when life is challenging. However, maintaining a grateful heart helps us to keep our eyes on God and to trust that He is working in our struggles. Romans 8:28 reminds us, "And we know that all things work together for good to them that love God, to them who are the called according to his purpose." Gratitude helps us to hold on to this promise, even when we can't see how things will work out. It reminds us that God is in control and is using our trials to refine our faith and accomplish His purposes. When we choose to be thankful, even in hardship, we express our trust in God's plan and belief that He is working all things together for our good.

Finally, gratitude is a form of worship. When we thank God for His blessings, we acknowledge His sovereignty and goodness. Psalm 92:1 says, "It is a good thing to give thanks unto the Lord, and to sing praises unto thy name, O most High." Thanksgiving is an act of worship that honors God and brings

Him glory. It is a way of saying, "God, I trust You. I believe You are good, and I am thankful for all You have done in my life." Gratitude draws us into a deeper relationship with God, helping us focus on His character and faithfulness. It shifts our attention away from our circumstances and onto the One who holds our lives in His hands. When we maintain a grateful heart, we live out our faith in a way that pleases God and brings Him glory.

In conclusion, maintaining a grateful heart is crucial for living a life that honors God and reflects His goodness. 1 Thessalonians 5:18 and Colossians 3:15 remind us to give thanks in all circumstances and let gratitude rule our hearts. Gratitude keeps us focused on God's goodness, helps us to trust in His provision, and fosters a sense of peace and joy, even in difficult times. It strengthens our relationship with God, builds our faith, and helps us see His hand at work. Gratitude also transforms our relationships with others, fostering connection, humility, and generosity. It protects us from bitterness and discontentment, helping us to find contentment in the blessings God has given us. Maintaining a grateful heart, we trust God's goodness, faithfulness, and sovereignty. Gratitude is a form of worship that honors God and brings Him glory, and it helps us to live with joy, peace, and contentment, no matter what life brings our way. Let us strive to maintain a grateful heart in all that we do, giving thanks to God for His endless blessings and His unchanging love.

Chapter 12 - Mission-Minded Living

Living a mission-minded life means understanding that, as Christians, we are called to live with a purpose beyond ourselves. It means knowing that we are called to be a light in the world, pointing others to Christ through our words, actions, and living. This is not just an option for those who feel a special calling to ministry or missionary work—this is the responsibility of every believer. Jesus' command in Matthew 28:19-20, known as the Great Commission, is clear: "Go ye therefore, and teach all nations, baptizing them in the name of the Father, and of the Son, and of the Holy Ghost: Teaching them to observe all things whatsoever I have commanded you." This charge was given to the disciples and all of His followers throughout time. It is a call to live with a mission, to share the gospel, make disciples, and show others the love of Christ.

Being mission-minded means seeing every moment, every interaction, and every relationship as an opportunity to share the good news of Jesus. It's about living with the awareness that we are ambassadors for Christ, representing Him to the world. In 2 Corinthians 5:20, Paul says, "Now then we are ambassadors for Christ, as though God did beseech you by us: we pray you in Christ's stead, be ye reconciled to God." As ambassadors, we are called to reflect Christ in everything we do, whether at school, at work, or in our communities. Our lives should testify to God's grace and love, drawing others to Him by how we live. This doesn't always mean preaching or directly talking about the gospel (though that is important, too), but it also means living in such a way that people can see the difference Christ has made in our lives.

One of the most critical aspects of mission-minded living is sharing the gospel. Romans 10:14 challenges us by asking, "How shall they believe in him of whom they have not heard? and how shall they hear without a preacher?" This verse reminds us that people cannot come to faith in Christ if they have never heard about Him. As followers of Jesus, we are called to share the gospel with those who have not heard or understood it. This can be done through conversations with friends, family, or even strangers and through acts of kindness that open the door for sharing God's love. Sharing the gospel doesn't have to be complicated—it can be as simple as telling someone about what Jesus has done in your life or explaining the basic message of salvation: that Jesus died for our sins, was buried, and rose again, and that through faith in Him, we can have eternal life.

However, living a mission-minded life is not just about what we say—it's also about how we live. Our actions often speak louder than words, and people watch how we live out our faith. Jesus said in Matthew 5:16, "Let your light so shine before men, that they may see your good works, and glorify your Father which is in heaven." When we live in a way that reflects Christ's love, kindness, humility, and forgiveness, we shine His light into the world. People will notice the difference in how we treat others, handle challenges, and live with integrity; they may be drawn to Christ because of how we live. This is why living with a mission mindset is essential, knowing that every day is an opportunity to reflect Christ to those around us.

Mission-minded living also requires us to build relationships with people who don't know Christ intentionally. It's easy to stay within our Christian circles, but Jesus calls us to go out and reach those lost. In Luke 19:10, Jesus said, "For the Son of man is come to seek and to save that which was lost." If Jesus came to seek out the lost, then we, as His followers, must do the same. This means stepping out of our comfort zones, engaging with people who may have different beliefs or lifestyles, and loving them just as Christ loves us. Building genuine relationships with non-believers opens the door for meaningful conversations about faith and creates opportunities to share the gospel naturally and relationally.

Another important aspect of being mission-minded is serving others. Jesus set an example for us by serving those around Him, even washing His disciples' feet as an act of humility and love. In Matthew 20:28, Jesus said, "Even as the Son of man came not to be ministered unto, but to minister, and to give his life a ransom for many." As His followers, we are called to serve others in the same way—humbly, sacrificially, and without expecting anything in return. When we serve others, whether through acts of kindness, volunteering, or simply helping someone in need, we show them Christ's love. Serving others is a powerful way to live out the gospel and to demonstrate the transformative power of God's love.

Being mission-minded also means being willing to sacrifice for the gospel's sake. Jesus made the ultimate sacrifice by giving His life for us, and while we may not be called to give our lives, we are called to sacrifice our time, resources, and comfort to further the kingdom of God. In Luke 9:23, Jesus said, "If any man will come after me, let him deny himself, and take up his cross daily, and follow me."

Living mission-minded requires us to deny ourselves—to put aside our desires and plans to follow God's will for our lives. This may mean sacrificing time to serve others, giving financially to support missions, or stepping out in faith to share the gospel with someone, even when it's uncomfortable.

Prayer is also a key component of mission-minded living. In Matthew 9:37-38, Jesus said, "The harvest truly is plenteous, but the labourers are few; Pray ye therefore the Lord of the harvest, that he will send forth labourers into his harvest." We are called to pray for those who are lost and for more people to be raised to share the gospel. Prayer is essential because it invites God to work in the hearts of those we are trying to reach and empowers us to be bold in sharing our faith. When we pray for the lost, we align our hearts with God's desire for everyone to come to know Him. Prayer also helps us to stay focused on our mission and reminds us that we are not doing this work in our strength but through the power of the Holy Spirit.

Mission-minded living is not just about what we do in our local communities—it also involves a global perspective. In Matthew 28:19, Jesus commands us to "Go ye therefore, and teach all nations,". This means that the gospel is not just for people in our neighborhoods or countries but for people worldwide. As Christians, we are called to have a heart for global missions, supporting missionaries, praying for the unreached, and being willing to go wherever God may lead us. Whether we are called to go overseas or to support global missions from where we are, we must remember that the Great Commission is an international mandate, and we all have a role to play in reaching the nations with the gospel.

Living mission-minded also means being prepared to face opposition and challenges. Jesus warned His followers that they would face persecution for His sake and promised to be with them. In John 16:33, Jesus said, "In the world ye shall have tribulation: but be of good cheer; I have overcome the world." When we live with a mission mindset, we may face rejection, criticism, or even persecution, but we can take heart knowing that Jesus has already overcome the world. Our mission is too critical to be derailed by fear or opposition. We are called to stand firm in our faith, trusting that God will give us the strength and courage to continue sharing His love, even in the face of adversity.

Being mission-minded also requires us to live with an eternal perspective. Colossians 3:2 says, "Set your affection on things above, not on things on the earth." When we live with eternity in mind, we realize that our time on earth is short and that what matters most is what we do for God's kingdom. Sharing the gospel and living in a way that points others to Christ has eternal significance. Every act of kindness, word of encouragement, and time we share the gospel matters because it can impact someone's eternity. Living with this perspective helps us to prioritize what's truly important and to stay focused on the mission God has given us.

Finally, mission-minded living is about hope. We share the gospel because Jesus is the world's hope. In 1 Peter 3:15, we are told, "But sanctify the Lord God in your hearts: and be ready always to give an answer to every man that asketh you a reason of the hope that is in you with meekness and fear." As followers of Christ, we have the hope of salvation, the hope of eternal life, and the hope of a relationship with God. This is the hope we are called to share with the world. When we live with a mission mindset, we share that hope with those who desperately need it, pointing them to the only One who can truly save and transform their lives.

In conclusion, mission-minded living means living with a purpose beyond ourselves. Matthew 28:19-20 and Romans 10:14 remind us that we are called to share the gospel and to live in a way that points others to Christ. This is not just the responsibility of a few—it is the calling of every believer. Mission-minded living involves sharing the gospel, building relationships with non-believers, serving others, sacrificing for the sake of the kingdom, praying for the lost, and living with an eternal perspective. It means being a light in the world, showing others the love of Christ through our words and actions. It also means being willing to face challenges and opposition, knowing that Jesus has already overcome the world. As we live mission-minded, we are fulfilling the Great Commission, bringing hope to lost people, and living for something that has eternal significance. Let us strive to live with a mission mindset, always ready to share the hope within us and make a difference for God's kingdom in the world around us.

Conclusion

As we conclude "Daughter of the King: Embracing Your Identity in Christ," remember that your journey with God doesn't end here. Every day is a new opportunity to grow deeper in your faith and live confidently as the daughter of the King. Embracing your identity in Christ means understanding that God profoundly loves, chooses, and empowers you. Life will have challenges, but knowing who you are in Him gives you the strength to face them with courage and grace. Just as a daughter trusts her father, continue to trust God with every step you take. Lean on His Word, stay connected in prayer, and surround yourself with others who will encourage your faith. Let the truth of your identity shape how you live, treat others, and pursue your dreams. When doubt or fear tries to creep in, remember that you belong to the One who created, redeemed, and called you His own. Take time to celebrate the victories, learn from the struggles, and always return to the arms of your Heavenly Father. As you move forward, seek to reflect Christ in all you do. You have a purpose, and your life can make a difference. Be bold, be brave, and be the daughter of the King God created you to be. Keep your eyes fixed on Jesus; He will guide you as you walk in His love and light. Never forget—your identity is secure in Him, now and forever.

Don't miss out!

Visit the website below and you can sign up to receive emails whenever Joshua Rhoades publishes a new book. There's no charge and no obligation.

https://books2read.com/r/B-A-AJLBB-ZVLAF

BOOKS 2 READ

Connecting independent readers to independent writers.

Did you love *Daughter Of The King: Embracing Your Identity In Christ*? Then you should read *Renewed Hope- How to Find Encouragement in God*[1] by Joshua Rhoades!

[2]

In a world where challenges and hardships seem to come at us from every side, it's easy to feel overwhelmed, discouraged, and even hopeless. We all face moments when we wonder how we will ever make it through the difficulties we encounter. But in these times, the Bible offers us a powerful example of finding strength and hope, no matter the circumstances. In 1 Samuel 30:6, we read about David, a man who faced great trials and overwhelming odds, yet in the midst of it all, "David encouraged himself in the LORD his God." This simple yet profound statement serves as the foundation for this book, "Renewed Hope- How to Find Encouragement in God." David's life was filled with ups and downs, moments of triumph and times of deep despair. He knew what it was like to be pursued by enemies, to experience loss, and to feel abandoned. Yet, even in his darkest hours, David found a way to renew his hope by turning to God. He didn't rely on his own strength or seek comfort in worldly solutions. Instead, he looked to the LORD, drawing strength and encouragement from his relationship with God. This book is an invitation to explore how we, too, can find renewed hope and encouragement in God, just as David did. It is a guide to understanding the power of faith, prayer, and trusting in God's promises, even when life seems unbearable. Throughout these pages, we will explore practical ways to draw closer

---

1. https://books2read.com/u/boeko1

2. https://books2read.com/u/boeko1

to God, to encourage ourselves in Him, and to discover the peace and strength that come from relying on the LORD. Whether you are facing a specific challenge right now or simply want to deepen your relationship with God, this book will provide you with the tools and inspiration you need to find encouragement in the LORD. As we journey together through the principles found in David's example, you will learn how to shift your focus from the problems that surround you to the God who sustains you. You will discover that no matter what life throws at you, there is always hope in the LORD, and by encouraging yourself in Him, you can face any situation with renewed strength and confidence. This is not just a book about surviving difficult times, but about thriving through them by finding your hope and encouragement in the unchanging character of God. So, whether you are struggling with personal challenges, feeling weighed down by the burdens of life, or simply seeking a deeper sense of peace and purpose, "Renewed Hope- How to Find Encouragement in God" is here to remind you that you are not alone, and that with God, there is always a reason to hope. Let David's example inspire you to turn to the LORD, to find your strength in Him, and to walk forward with a renewed sense of hope, no matter what you face.